W9-BOO-845

The Frog in the Pond

and Other
Animal Stories

Children's Press ®
An Imprint of Scholastic Inc.
New York • Toronto • London • Auckland • Sydney
Mexico City • New Delhi • Hong Kong
Danbury, Connecticut

Dear Rookie Reader,

Do you like animals?
Then this is the book for you!

Meet two **funny** pets.
Meet a frog and a fish, too.

Have fun and keep reading!

P.S. Don't forget to check
out the fun activities on
pages 124–127.

Get Out of My Chair

By Kathy Schulz
Illustrated by Tom Payne

Get out of my chair.

Go on your way.

Get out of my chair.

You cannot stay.

Get out of my chair.
I am telling you.

Get out of my chair.
I will count to two.

Get out of my chair.
You must get down.

Get out of my chair,
you little clown.

Get out of my chair.
Listen, Rover!

Get out of my chair . . .

or scoot over.

Old Mo

By Stacey W. Hsu

Illustrated by Adam Ritter

I have a cat.

His name is Mo.

His nose is cold.

His green eyes glow!

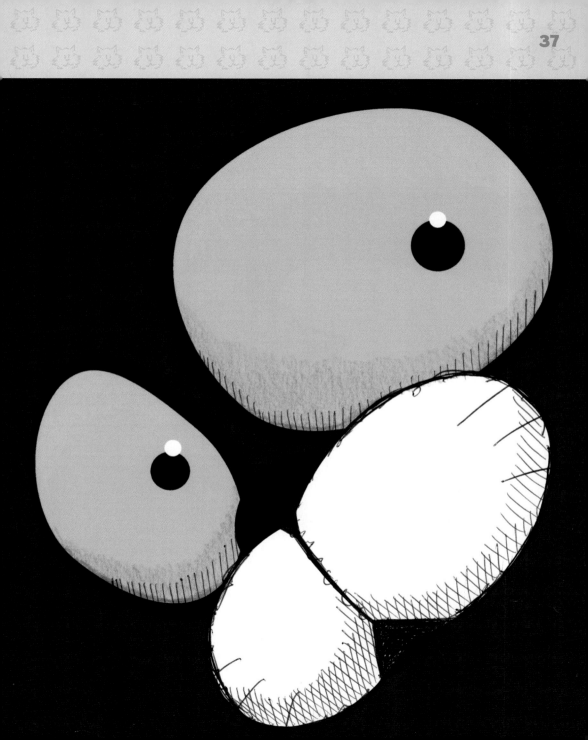

He flops on beds.

He flops on chairs.

He flops on me.

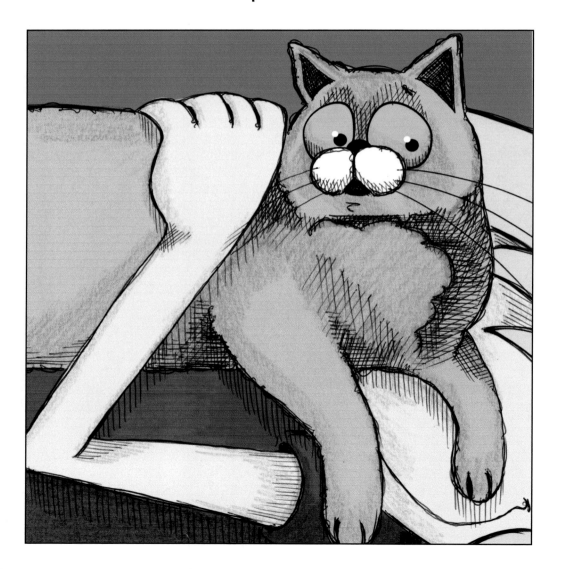

He flops on stairs.

He purrs really loudly.

He loves to sing.

He chases birds and
other things.

He sleeps all day.

He prowls all night.

He loves to play.

He never bites.

I love old Mo.
He loves me too.

This is how he tells me,
"Mew!"

The Frog in the Pond

By Wil Mara

Illustrated by Cheryl Mendenhall

Yesterday,
I found a frog in the pond
behind my house!

It seemed like a very happy frog.

It sat on a log and croaked.

Suddenly, an ugly bug crawled in front of the frog.

The frog leaned down
and snapped it up!

I decided to keep the frog.
I took it off the log
and brought it inside.

I put the frog in a tank with a rock and some water.

I watched the frog all day
and all night.

I gave the frog some
more bugs to eat.

But the frog did not eat the bugs.
It even stopped croaking!

The frog seemed sad.

The frogs in the pond seemed
to like being together.
Did my frog miss its friends?

Today, I brought the frog back
to the pond and let it go.

The frog hopped on a log and started croaking. It even ate a bug that was crawling by.

The frog was happy again.
I was happy too!

One Smart Fish

By Laura Manivong

Illustrated by Suzanne Beaky

I want to catch a fish to eat.

I bait my hook with hot dog meat.

I cast my line. I hold my reel.
I wait there for my tasty meal.

I get no bites. I check my hook.
The hot dog's gone.

The wind picks up.
Clouds roll in.

I hear a plop.

I spy a fin.

It starts to rain but I won't go.
I bait my line with cookie dough.

I feel a twitch.
I check once more.

He stole again, just like before!

I have a trick. That fish won't win.

I'll stick my bait on a safety pin.

I hook on Grandpa's prized spaghetti.

I'm robbed again!
I quit already!

That fish is smarter than I knew.
What did I catch? A cold! ACHOO!

Match each word with its rhyme.

over	**clown**
way	**two**
you	**Rover**
down	**stay**

Now make your own rhymes!
What rhymes with chair?

Pick the right word.
Finish this sentence.

Mo has green_____.
eyes   nose   ears

What else is green?

These pictures are all mixed up!
What happened first?
What happened next?
What happened last?

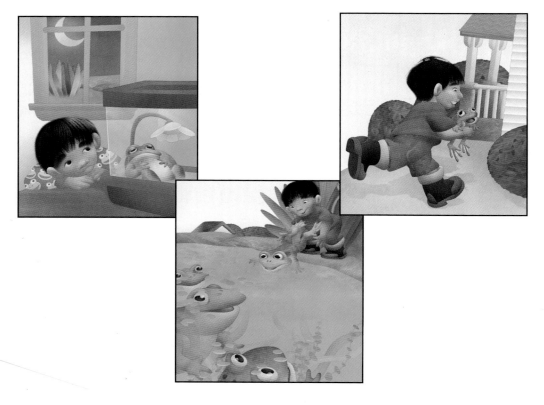

hat was the best part of the story?

Match the words and pictures.

spaghetti
hot dog
cookie dough

What happened when the fish
saw these foods?

What would you use to catch a fish?

Library of Congress Cataloging-in-Publication Data

The frog in the pond and other animal stories.
   p. cm. -- (A Rookie reader treasury)
  Contents: Get out of my chair / by Kathy Schulz ; illustrated by Tom Payne
            Old Mo / by Stacey W. Hsu ; illustrated by Adam Ritter
            The Frog in the Pond / by Wil Mara ; illustrated by Cheryl Mendenhall
            One Smart Fish / by Laura Manivong ; illustrated by Suzanne Beaky.
    ISBN-13: 978-0-531-21727-6
    ISBN-10: 0-531-21727-2

 1. Children's stories, American. [1. Short stories.]
I. Title. II. Series.

PZ5F91752 2008
[E]--dc22   2008008296

Cover top right, TOC top left, and illustrations pages 5-27, 124 © 2001 Tom Payne
Cover bottom left, TOC top right, and illustrations pages 29-59, 125 © 2006 Adam Ritter
Cover top left, TOC bottom left, and illustrations pages 61-91, 126 © 2007 Cheryl Mendenhall
Cover bottom right, TOC bottom right, and illustrations pages 93-123, 127 © 2006 Suzanne Beaky